How have things changed?

In the Town

James Nixon

First published in 2008 by
Franklin Watts
338 Euston Road
London NW1 3BH

Franklin Watts Australia
Level 17/207 Kent Street
Sydney NSW 2000

ISBN: 978 0 7496 7845 6

Dewey classification number: 307.76

A CIP catalogue record for this book is available from the British Library.

Planning and production by Discovery Books Limited
Editor: James Nixon
Designer: Ian Winton

Photographs: p6 Courtesy of Derbyshire Times and www.picturethepast. org.uk, p7 Bobby Humphrey, p8 Mary Evans Picture Library, p9 Bobby Humphrey, p10-11 Chris Fairclough, p12 (top) Mary Evans Picture Library, p12 (bottom) Severn Trent Water, p13 Chris Fairclough, p14 Getty Images, p15 Chris Fairclough, p16 (top) Courtesy of Nottingham City Council and www.picturethepast.org.uk, p16 (bottom) Getty Images, p17 (top) Bobby Humphrey, p17 (middle) Chris Fairclough, p17 (bottom) Sainsbury's, p18 (top) Mary Evans Picture Library, p18 (bottom) The Francis Frith Collection, p19 Bobby Humphrey, p20 Mary Evans Picture Library, p21 (top) Chris Fairclough, p21 (bottom) Bobby Humphrey, p22 Mary Evans Picture Library, p23 Bobby Humphrey, p24 (top) Mary Evans Picture Library, p24 (bottom) Getty Images, p25 (top) Chris Fairclough, p25 (bottom) Jacqueline Abromeit/ istockphoto.com, p26 (top) Getty Images, p26 (bottom) Bobby Humphrey, p27 (top) Courtesy of Nottingham City Council and www.picturethepast.org.uk, p27 (bottom) Notts County Football Club.

Cover photos: (top) Courtesy of Derbyshire Times and www.picturethepast.org.uk, (bottom) Bobby Humphrey.

Printed in China

Franklin Watts is a division of Hachette Children's Books, an Hachette Livre UK company
www.hachettelivre.co.uk

Contents

How have towns changed?

The towns that we live in have been through many changes over time. Towns are still changing today. Towns grow bigger as new houses and **businesses** are built on the outskirts.

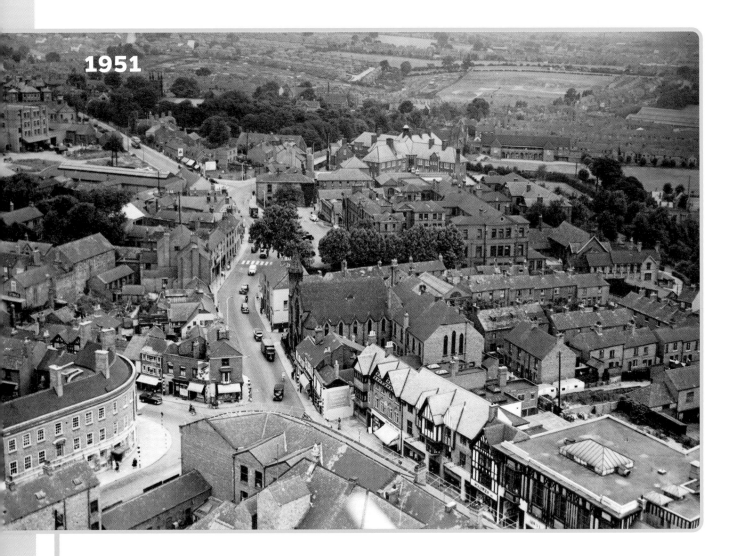

1951

This bird's-eye view of Chesterfield shows what the town was like in 1951.

Look at this recent photograph of Chesterfield and compare it to the one on the opposite page. You can see how fast the town has grown in the last 60 years.

Now

Some of the fields in the distance have been built on. Many of the buildings in the town centre have disappeared. Can you see what the car parks in the modern picture have replaced?

Then and now

What buildings in the old picture still exist today?

In Victorian times lots of cheap **terraced** houses were built for the factory workers in the city centres.

These houses were packed in tightly together with no gardens between them.

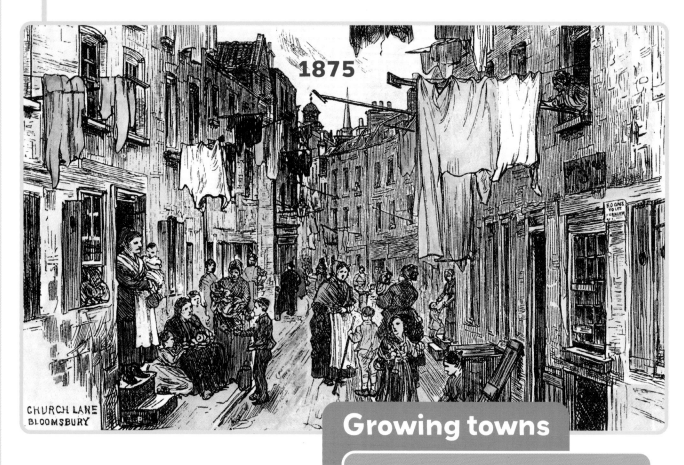

1875

CHURCH LANE
BLOOMSBURY

Large families often had to live in just one or two rooms. Toilets and running water were shared by several houses in the street.

Growing towns

During the **Industrial Revolution** huge numbers of people moved to the towns and cities to find work. By 1851 over half of the population were living in **urban** areas.

Many Victorian terraces like these are still lived in today but they have been **modernised.**

How can you tell that some houses in this photo have had extra rooms added into the roof?

Other terraces have been cleared and replaced with modern houses or blocks of flats. A lot of the old factories have also been knocked down to make way for new homes in the city centre.

Homes in the suburbs

Towns grow as homes and businesses are built on their edges. These areas are called the **suburbs**.

In Victorian times some wealthy people left the city centres to live in suburbs like the one below.

The suburbs were pleasant areas to live, with trees and big houses set back from the street.

Why has this house been built without a place to park a car?

You can still see the big Victorian homes in towns today, but many are no longer on the edge of town. New homes, shops and factories have been built further out.

Here is a typical modern suburban estate. There is enough space for each house to have its own garage and driveway.

How many cars do you think there is room to park at this house?

Public health

In Victorian times living conditions in big towns and cities were not good.

Crowded **slums** like the one in this picture were very unhealthy. Rubbish was usually thrown out into the street. **Sewage** flowed through open ditches. In these conditions many diseases spread.

1852

From 1875 workers began to build a network of sewer pipes under the streets of every town. The sewers took waste water away from every building.

1908

What do you think the workman in this photo is doing?

Today, nobody lives like the poor did in the Victorian slums. Clean water is now brought to us through underground pipes. Dirty water is taken down drains into the sewers.

Local **councils** employ workers to keep the streets tidy.

See if you can find evidence of the sewers near your house. Under this Victorian manhole cover is a way down for workers to inspect the sewers.

Workplaces

Britain became wealthy by making things to sell around the world. Massive factories produced goods like steel and cotton. Other towns had coal mines or built great ships.

1957

This picture from 1957 shows workers in a Lancashire town heading off for a day's work in the cotton **mill**. Sometimes whole towns relied on one factory.

How do you think a town would be affected if a big factory closed down?

Since the 1970s many factories have closed down. Some of the buildings have been knocked down or turned into something else. This old mill has been turned into the offices of a local newspaper.

There are still some big factories in Britain, but today more people work in offices. Places of work are often now built away from the town centre on industrial estates like this one.

Why is it good for workplaces to be built together on the edge of town?

Shops

Most of the shops in towns were a lot smaller in the 1920s than they are today.

Shops were usually found in and around the high street in a town centre.

Look at these shops in Nottingham town centre in 1928.

1928

1940

Each shop would sell a particular product like this fishmonger. Food shopping took a lot longer then because lots of different shops had to be visited.

Now

Look at Nottingham town centre today. Most shops are much larger and some sell lots of different things.

Then and now

Would you prefer to go shopping in the past or today? Why?

Many shops in the big town centres have moved off the street into indoor shopping centres like this one.

You can now do all your food shopping under one roof in a supermarket. Supermarkets and other stores are often built on the edge of the town.

Parks

By 1900 the **government** had opened parks in many towns. These gave people living in the crowded slums

1900

GREENWICH PARK

clean and open spaces to use. These Victorians are sitting in Greenwich Park in London.

1902

Most people then did not have transport to get out of town, so the park was perfect for a day out.

Then and now

Look at the pram the young girl is pushing and compare it to the pram in the modern picture on the right.

People still enjoy going to Greenwich Park today.

Now

Then and now

Parks are a good place to go for a walk or to play sports such as football and cricket. Quiet, open spaces such as parks have become even more important as towns have become busier.

What can the child with the telescope see that is not in the picture of the park in 1900?

Transport

Over a hundred years ago people lived close to the shops and their place of work. As towns grew bigger, people had to travel further to work or shop.

1895

In this old photo of New Street in Birmingham's town centre people are using horse-drawn transport such as carts and carriages. There were even horse-drawn buses and trams at this time but there was not as much traffic on the roads.

Today, nearly everybody owns a motor car. The roads in town are full of traffic and it can be expensive to park. It is often easier to cycle or to use the bus or tram.

Many busy centres of town, like Birmingham New Street pictured below have been **pedestrianised** so people can shop safely.

What problems are there with heavy traffic in towns? In what ways can we reduce the amount of traffic in towns?

Now

21

Street furniture

Street furniture is all the objects fixed in the street such as traffic lights, phone boxes and bus shelters.

Look at this photo taken on the corner of Corporation Road and Gurney Street in Middlesbrough in 1913. There was not much street furniture then. There were gas lamps in a town street but not much else.

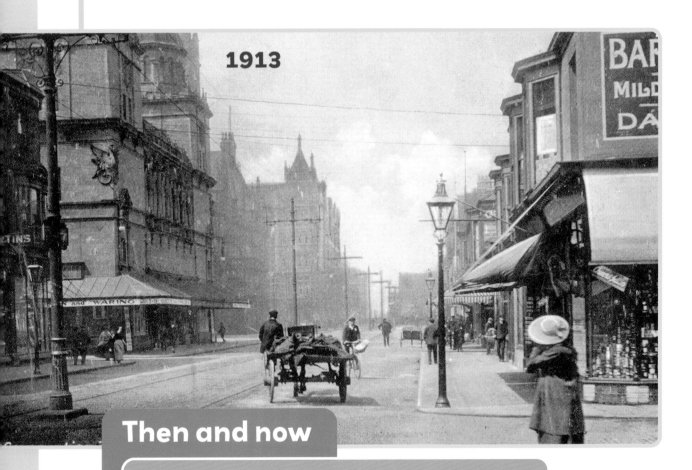

1913

BAR
MILD
DA

Then and now

Look at the street then and now on the two pages. Can you find the following:
- bus shelter
- gas lamp
- electric lamp
- litter bin
- bollards
- road signs

As roads have got busier, more and more street furniture has appeared. Look at all the objects in Corporation Road today.

Now

The road signs help drivers find where they are going or warn them of hazards ahead. Pedestrians can make use of the information post, litter bins and benches.

What vehicle other than a motorcycle could you park by these railings?

Lighting

Until the 1930s few towns had electricity. Homes had candles and gas lamps but these were put out when people went to bed.

The only lights in the town at night came from the gas lamps in the street. They had to be lit by a man every evening and put out every morning. Some streets without lamps would be completely dark.

1896

1933

In the 1930s a network of **cables** and **pylons** was built to bring electricity to every town. Gas lamps were gradually replaced by electric street lights.

Today every street in the town is lit up and electric lights shine out from people's homes and shops. Street lights now come on automatically when it gets dark. This street has been decorated with lights for Christmas.

Look out for neon signs next time you are in the town centre at night. These lights come in different colours.

Places of entertainment

At the beginning of the twentieth century people had less time for leisure activities. However people did go to the theatre to watch plays, musicals or pantomimes.

Music halls were popular with ordinary working people. This one in London's Leicester Square was called the Alhambra. It provided a mixture of drama, songs and comedy acts.

1936

Now

The Alhambra music hall was knocked down in 1936 and replaced with this cinema. Most towns now have a cinema. People spend more time having fun today. A town may also have a bowling alley, a swimming pool and a football stadium.

1927

Football grounds

Watching sports events has grown in popularity since the late Victorian times. Football stadiums have got bigger and bigger over the years. Look at Notts County's ground in 1927 and compare it to now.

Now

What happened to fans at the old ground when it rained?

Businesses Groups of people that work together to make or sell things.

Cables Thick wires used for carrying electricity from one place to another.

Council The local government that runs a region of a country.

Government The people who rule a country.

Industrial Revolution The period in Britain's history when lots of factories were built and production of goods increased at a fast rate. It happened in the late eighteenth century and nineteenth century.

Mill A large factory containing machinery for the production of goods such as cotton or paper.

Modernised Made more modern or up-to-date.

Pedestrianised Closed to vehicles – made into a place where you can only travel through on foot.

Pylons Tall structures that are used for supporting cables above the ground.

Sewage Dirty water and waste that is carried away from buildings.

Slums Overcrowded or poor areas of housing.

Suburbs Areas on the edge of a town or city.

Terraced Describes houses that are joined together.

Urban To do with towns or cities.

Places to visit:

Find out at the **local museum** or the **local library** the history of your town. You may find old photographs of the town at these places. You might also find maps from the past that will show you how the town has grown over the years.

Ironbridge Gorge Museum, Shropshire (www.ironbridge.org.uk). Here you can learn about the changes that took place in industry, transport and public health during the Industrial Revolution. These changes explain how small villages exploded into large towns.

Most cities have a museum of their history. Examples are:
Museum of Edinburgh (www.cac.org.uk)
Leeds City Museum (opens August 2008)
Cardiff Museum (www.museumwales.ac.uk)
Museum of London (www.museumoflondon.org.uk)

Websites:

There are many websites where you can view historical photos of town life. You may even find old photos of places you know. Try the website of your **local council** and see if they have an image gallery.

www.francisfrith.com
has historical images of most towns in the UK

www.picturethepast.org.uk
has a large database of old photographs taken in the East Midlands

www.gtj.org.uk
for old photos of towns in Wales

Books to read:

Britain in Victorian Times, Tim Locke, 2003 (Franklin Watts)
Four Great Cities: Then and Now, Margaret Lysecki, 2004 (Longman)
History Snapshots series, Sarah Ridley, 2007 (Franklin Watts)
Step-up Geography: Local Traffic – an Environmental Issue, Julia Roche, 2006 (Evans)
Then and Now, Jenny Vaughan, 2004 (Longman)
Where You Live series, Ruth Nason, 2007 (Franklin Watts)

Index